Duden

kurz geübt & schnell kapiert

Englischheft

7. Klasse

Dudenverlag
Berlin

Lernplan von _____

5

Adverbien der Art und Weise

Adjektive (*adjectives*) beschreiben Personen und Sachen.
Adverbien (*adverbs*) beschreiben Tätigkeiten. Viele Adverbien der Art und
Weise werden gebildet, indem **an das Adjektiv ein -ly angehängt** wird.
Beispiel: *A **bad** singer is someone who sings **badly**.*
      adjective   *verb* *adverb*

1 Write down the adverbs to these adjectives.

adjective	adverb		adjective	adverb
polite	*politely*		impolite	
clear			unclear	
comfortable			uncomfortable	
happy			unhappy	
quiet			noisy	
quick			slow	
careful			careless	

13

2 You visited two different restaurants and now you take some notes.
Complete the following sentences. Use the adverbs from exercise 1.

1. In "The Happy Snacks" the waiters talked *politely*.

2. The food came _____.

3. The customers sat _____.

4. The band played _____.

5. The waiters served the food _____.

6. The waiter wrote the menu _____ so it was easy to read.

7. There was a menu for children so they ate their food _____.

8. In "Mother's Kitchen" the waiters talked _____.

9. The food came _____.

10. The customers sat _____.

11. The band played _____.

12. The waiters served the food _____.

13. The waiter wrote the menu _____ so it was

   difficult to read.

14. There was nothing special on the menu for the children so they

   ate their food _____ | 13

   26 – 22 Punkte  21 – 14 Punkte  13 – 0 Punkte  Gesamt-punktzahl

Adverbien: Komparativ und Superlativ

Adverbien mit zwei oder mehr Silben, also auch Adverbien, die auf -ly enden, werden mit **more** (*comparative*) und **most** (*superlative*) gesteigert, z. B.:
*She did her homework reluctant**ly*****. Her brother did it even **more** reluctantly.
They do their maths homework **most** reluctantly.*

Adverbien, die dieselbe Form haben wie das Adjektiv, also auch alle ein-silbigen Adverbien, werden mit **-er** bzw. **-est** gesteigert, z. B.:
*Jamie speaks fast. Sarah speaks fast**er** than Jamie. Ben speaks fast**est**.*

Early / earlier / earliest ist das einzige Adverb mit der Endung -ly, das nicht mit *more* bzw. *most* gesteigert wird. Warum?
Weil Adjektiv und Adverb die gleiche Form haben: *early.*

* *reluctantly* = widerwillig

1 Write down the names of the countries next to their flags.
Do you know which languages are spoken in these countries?
Write them down next to the names.
Tipp: Denke daran, dass Ländernamen, Nationalitäten und Sprachen im Englischen immer großgeschrieben werden.

	country	language
	1. *Great Britain*	*English*
	2. _____	_____
	3. _____	_____
	4. _____	_____
	5. _____	_____
	6. _____	_____

7. _____   _____

8. _____   _____ | 14 |

1

2 **Write sentences using the words given. You have to use the comparative adverb form.**

1. German drivers / to drive / aggressively / than Swedish drivers.

   German drivers drive more aggressively than Swedish drivers.

2. French trains / to go / fast / than Italian trains.

   _____

3. The English / to look after their gardens / carefully / than the French.

   _____

4. Most French people / to eat / exquisitely / than the English.

   _____

5. The Italians / to relax / easily / than the Swiss.

   _____

6. Japanese people / to speak / quietly / than Italians.

   _____

7. Germans / to talk / slowly / than the French.

   _____ | 6 |

/

     **20 – 17 Punkte**    **16 – 11 Punkte**    **10 – 0 Punkte**    **Gesamt-punktzahl**

Possessivpronomen

Possessivpronomen (*possessive pronouns*) **ersetzen Possessivbegleiter**
(*possessive determiners*) **+ Nomen** (*noun*).
Dadurch werden Sätze kürzer und man kann Wiederholungen vermeiden,
z. B.: *Where is my book? Oh, you are reading mine (= my book).*
   Where is yours (= your book)?

my + noun	*mine*		*our + noun*	*ours*
your + noun	*yours*		*your + noun*	*yours*
his + noun	*his*		*their + noun*	*theirs*
her + noun	*hers*			
its + noun	*its*			

1 **Louise, Liz, Lorraine, Linda, Lorretta and Lucia are sisters. Louise and Liz are twins. The six sisters try to find their presents under the Christmas tree. Help them and complete the conversation on page 9.**

Lorretta

Lorraine

Louise & Liz

Lucia

Linda

Louise & Liz

8

1. Lucia: "Wow, I think the present with the white bow is *mine*."

2. Louise: "Hey Liz! I don't think it's _____. Do you think the

   white present is for Lucia?"

3. Liz: "No, it's not _____. Listen Lucia, the white present is not

   _____ . _____ is the black one! The white present is for

   Linda, it's _____!"

4. Lucia: "OK, OK the twins know it all ... Which one is for them?

   Which present is _____?"

5. Lorraine: "The pink one is _____. It has got their name on it."

6. Louise & Liz: "No, the red present is _____!"

7. Lorraine: "Calm down! They are both _____, the red one and

   the pink one."

8. Lorretta: "Hm, let me see. There must be a computer screen somewhere.

   Here, the green present is _____."

9. Lucia: "Lorraine, which one is _____?"

10. Lorraine: "The green present is _____. I know what it is: it's a chair."

11. Louise: "Oh, here is an African drum! Whose drum is that?

    Is it _____, Lucia? It is wonderful!"

12. Lucia: "Yes, the drum is _____. I love it! What did you get?"

13. Liz & Louise: "The bike is _____ and the saddle is _____, too."

16

2

  16–13 **Punkte**  12–8 **Punkte**  7–0 **Punkte**   Gesamt-punktzahl

Reflexivpronomen

Reflexivpronomen beziehen sich auf das **Subjekt des Satzes**, z. B.:

Ben hurt **himself**.
The machine switches **itself** off automatically.
"Do **you** pay for **yourselves**?" – "Yes, **we** pay for **ourselves**."
"You see: **They** pay for **themselves**!"

myself	mir/mich	*ourselves*	uns
yourself	dir/dich	*yourselves*	euch
himself	sich	*themselves*	sich
herself	sich		
itself	sich		

Achtung: ***each other*** heißt „sich (gegenseitig)" und nicht „sich (selbst)":
Tina is smiling at herself.   *Sue and Jim are smiling at each other.*

1 **Look at the conversation and write the correct reflexive pronoun in the blanks.**

Josh: "Look, here's an interesting book. Now I'll be able to teach

_____ German!" Hannah: "Are you joking? You want to teach

_____ German?" Jamie: "Hey Sarah! Josh wants to teach

_____ German!" Sarah: "Well, that's great. I think we should do

that, too. Jamie, can we all teach _____ German?"

Josh: "I can think for _____, so you two will be able to think for _____, too. I bought this book for _____

and you surely can buy it for _____, too. So I think we all

should be able to teach _____ German, shouldn't we?"

Jamie: "You speak for _____ , Josh. I don't know if I can really

teach _____ German or anything else." Josh: "Don't worry!

The book is very easy: It explains *itself*. We will be there to help you, too." | 11 |

2

★ **2** **Write sentences with reflexive pronouns or "each other".**

1. Alan / to cut / with his knife / yesterday

   Alan cut himself with his knife yesterday.

2. Cats / to clean / every day

   _____

3. Ben and Josh / to talk / yesterday

   _____

4. Usually / I / to repair / my bike

   _____

5. Jamie and Sarah / to help / with their homework / every day

   _____

6. Hannah / to look at / in the mirror / every morning

   _____ | 5 |

  16 – 13 **Punkte**  12 – 8 **Punkte**  7 – 0 **Punkte**   **Gesamt-punktzahl**

Modale Hilfsverben

Modal auxiliaries (modale Hilfsverben) gibt es in der Regel nur im *present tense*. Sie haben keine Partizipien (*-ing-* oder *-ed*-Form) und keinen Infinitiv. Für Zeiten wie das *simple past* und das Futur müssen deswegen **Ersatzverben** benutzt werden.

modal auxiliary	Ersatzverb	past	future
I can do it. (Ich kann das.)	*to be able to* (können)	*I was able to do it.*	*I will be able to do it.*
I can't / cannot do it. (Ich kann das nicht.)	*not to be able to* (nicht können)	*I could not do it.** I was not able to do it.*	*I won't be able to do it.*
We can* go. (Wir dürfen gehen.)	*to be allowed to* (dürfen)	*We were allowed to go.*	*We will be allowed to go.*
We mustn't go. (Wir dürfen nicht gehen.)	*not to be allowed to* (nicht dürfen)	*We were not allowed to go.*	*We won't be allowed to go.*
Ben must / has to work. (Ben muss arbeiten.)	*to have to* (müssen)	*Ben had to work.*	*Ben will have to work.*
You needn't / don't have to work. (Du musst nicht arbeiten.)	*not to have to* (nicht müssen)	*You didn't have to work.*	*You won't have to work.*

*   In sehr höflichen Sätzen kann statt *can* auch *may* stehen.
** Ausnahmsweise hat das modale Hilfsverb *can* auch eine Vergangenheitsform: *could*.

Achtung: Die verneinte Form von *must* (= muss) ist *needn't* (= muss nicht / braucht nicht) und nicht *mustn't* (= darf nicht). *Mustn't* (= darf nicht) ist eine mögliche Verneinung zu *can*.

Alan has moved* recently. He describes the way to his new address to Jim.

Alan: "You must take the number 8 to Heather Green. You can take the number 5 bus and then the number 7 bus, but it takes longer. Get off at Colin's Chip Shop. You mustn't get off at the cinema because then you must walk much further. From Colin's Chip Shop you must only walk for about five minutes. You can see the back of our house from the bus stop but you mustn't climb over the garden fence. You needn't walk along the road. You can walk through the park – it's quicker. If you can't find your way you can phone me and I can pick you up** at the phone box. You needn't buy a return ticket: My father can take you home by car."
It was difficult for Jim to find Alan's new address. He made a few mistakes. He didn't do what Alan said. Here is what Jim thought:
Jim: "I must take the number 5 and then number 7. I must get off at the cinema. I must walk along the road. I mustn't climb over the garden fence. I must walk through the park. I must buy a return ticket."

* to move = umziehen   ** to pick somebody up = jemanden abholen

1 Now write on an extra piece of paper what Jim was supposed to do. **Start like this:**

Jim had to take the number 8. He had to get off at Colin's ...

pro richtiges Prädikat 1 Punkt   11

★ **2** The next time Jim visits Alan he won't make any mistakes. Complete the following sentences. Use modal auxiliaries in the future tense.

1. The next time I *will have to take* the number 8 bus.

2. I _____ get off at Colin's Chip Shop. 3. From Colin's Chip

Shop I _____ for five minutes. 4. From the bus stop I

_____ to see the back of Alan's house. 5. I _____

buy a return ticket. 6. Alan's father _____ to take me home.   5

13

  16 – 13 Punkte  **12 – 8 Punkte**  **7 – 0 Punkte**  **Gesamt-punktzahl**

Das Gerundium

Here's what Jim and his friends like and what they don't like.

	to love / to enjoy	to like	to dislike	to hate
Jim	eat spaghetti	play football	wash the dishes	do homework
Tina	play computer games	go to the cinema	read books	play football
Bob	read books	play the piano	go shopping	play football
Sue	go swimming	go to pop concerts	learn vocabulary	ride horses

1 **Make sentences. When there is a question mark write down the answer, too.**

1. Jim / spaghetti *Jim loves eating spaghetti.*

2. Tina / football? *Does Tina like playing football? No, she hates playing football.*

3. Tina / cinema _____

4. Sue / swimming _____

5. Jim / dishes? _____

_____

6. Bob / piano _____

7. Sue / horses _____

8. Bob / books? _____

_____

9. Tina / computer games _____

10. Sue / pop concerts? _____

_____

11. Bob / shopping _____

12. Sue / vocabulary _____

pro richtigen Satz 1 Punkt ☐ 13

3

2 **Write down what the boys and girls like or dislike. Use the verbs given.**

to watch   *to play*   *to eat*   *to go*

| Jim | Tina | Bob | Sue |

Jim _____

Tina _____

Bob _____

Sue _____ ☐ 4

15

Das Gerundium als Subjekt und Objekt

> Das *gerund* kann als Nomen Subjekt eines Satzes sein, z. B.:
> **Collecting** CDs can be very expensive.

1 Sarah wants to have a party. Write down her plans and use the gerund as the subject of the sentences.

	yes (necessary)	no (unnecessary / stupid)
1. to write invitations		✘ (can phone)
2. to play party games		✘ (too old)
3. to move furniture	✘ (need room to dance)	
4. to make a cake		✘ (Mum is baking one)
5. to organize music	✘ (haven't got enough CDs)	
6. to buy candles	✘ (make great light)	

1. *Writing invitations is unnecessary as I can phone everybody.*

2. _____ *is stupid. We are too old for these things.*

3. _____

_____

4. _____

_____

5. _____

_____

6. _____

_____

5

Auch Verben, die auf eine Präposition (z. B. *of, in, at, about*) folgen, stehen im *gerund*. Oft kommt das *gerund* nach Ausdrücken wie diesen vor:
to be good at – etwas gut können; *to be afraid of* – vor etwas Angst haben;
to be tired of – auf etwas keine Lust mehr haben; *to be interested in* – sich für etwas interessieren, z. B.:
*Sue **is good at swimming**. But she **is afraid of swimming** in the sea.*

2 **Write sentences and practise the gerund.**

1. Bob / to be tired of / to cycle

   Bob is _____

2. Mrs Pott / to be very interested in / to buy clothes

   _____

3. Jamie / to be crazy about / to climb mountains

   _____

4. Some dogs / to be not afraid of / to jump into the water

   _____

5. Hannah / to be good at / to write stories

   _____

6. Josh / to be bad at / to play chess

   _____

7. Mr Brown / to be famous for / to run 100 metres in 11 seconds

   _____ | 7 |

3

 | | 12 – 10 **Punkte**  9 – 7 **Punkte**  6 – 0 **Punkte**  | | Gesamt- punktzahl

Verben mit zwei Objekten

Einige Verben *(z. B. to bring, to give, to buy, to tell)* können zwei Objekte haben: ein direktes und ein indirektes Objekt.
Das **indirekte Objekt** ist meist eine Person, das **direkte Objekt** ist meist eine Sache. Oft steht das indirekte Objekt vor dem direkten Objekt, z. B.:

Sarah gives   *Josh*   *a postcard of the castle.*
                    indirektes Objekt   direktes Objekt

Ändert sich die Reihenfolge der Objekte, wird **to** oder **for** eingefügt, z. B.:
*Sarah gives a postcard of the castle **to** Josh.*
*Ben buys a CD **for** Jamie.*

1 Underline the direct object with a <u>continuous line</u> and the indirect object with a <u>broken line</u> in these sentences.

1. Alan bought <u>a souvenir from Wales</u> for his mother.
2. The guide tells the tourists the history of the castle.
3. I will send all my friends postcards.
4. The waiter will bring a cup of tea for us.
5. "Give your camera to me!"
6. The man offered the tourists photos of the ghost.
7. In the end he sold more than 20 photos to the tourists.

12

2 Change these sentences. Put the indirect object first.

1. "Give the map of the town to Jim!"

   _____

2. My father tells the story of the castle to the group of visitors.

   _____

3. Our teacher wanted to buy tickets for a sightseeing tour for the class.

   _____

4. The cook made soup for them.

_____

5. My mother asked me to bring a T-shirt from Wales for her.

_____ | 5 |

★ **3** **Translate the following sentences into English.**

1. Der Lehrer gab den Schülern Texte über (= *on*) Wales.

_____

2. Ich schickte zwei Postkarten an meine Freunde.

_____

3. Die Touristen kauften ihren Freunden viele Andenken (= *souvenirs*).

_____

4. Der Reiseführer (= *the guide*) zeigte den Touristen den Weg.

_____

5. Meine Mutter hat James ein T-Shirt gekauft.

_____

6. Ben schrieb seiner Schwester drei E-Mails (= *emails*).

_____

7. „Bitte bringen Sie mir eine Tasse Kaffee.“

_____ | 7 |

3

  24 – 19 Punkte  18 – 13 Punkte  12 – 0 Punkte  Gesamt-punktzahl

simple present / present progressive

Das **simple present** entspricht dem Infinitiv bei Vollverben, außer in der 3. Person Singular, denn da gilt: „*He, she, it* – ein „s" muss mit!"
Das *simple present* drückt **Vorgänge** aus, die **immer oder nie, regelmäßig oder normalerweise** geschehen und wird sehr oft mit den folgenden Zeitangaben benutzt:
every day/month/year, on Mondays/Tuesdays ... (= jeden Montag ...),
always, never, often, sometimes, usually, normally.

Das **present progressive** wird gebildet aus einer Personalform von *to be* und dem Infinitiv + *-ing* (= Partizip Präsens). Das *present progressive* drückt **Vorgänge** aus, die **jetzt gerade, in diesem Augenblick** geschehen, und wird sehr oft mit den folgenden Zeitangaben benutzt:
now, at the moment, at present, today/this week/this month.

MONDAY	6 a.m. indoor swimming pool
TUESDAY	do special stretching programme
WEDNESDAY	no training
THURSDAY	swim 3,000 m with Sally
FRIDAY	train for 100 m distance
SATURDAY	run 6 miles with Mum
SUNDAY	no sports

1 **Sue is very good at swimming. She is in a swimming club. Look at her diary and write down what she does every day.**

Sue (to get up) _____ at 5 o'clock on Mondays because she

(to go) _____ to the indoor swimming pool. She (to do)

_____ a special training programme every Tuesday. Usually there (not to be) _____ any training on Wednesdays. Sue and her friend

Sally always (to swim) _____ 3,000 metres on Thursdays.

On Fridays Sue (to train) _____ for the 100 metre distance.

On Saturdays she and her mother (to run) _____ 6 miles.   7

2   **Sue has won a competition. A reporter interviews her. Fill in the right forms of the simple present or the present progressive.**

Reporter: "Hello, Sue. Congratulations! What does your training programme look like?"

Sue: "Thank you. I (to do) _____ a lot of training during the week. But

I also (to have) _____ time to relax. On Wednesdays and Sundays I

(not to do) _____ any sports. On Mondays I (to go) _____ to

the indoor swimming pool and on Thursdays my friend Sally (to swim)

_____ 3,000 metres with me. On Saturdays my mother (to run)

_____ 6 miles with me. We always (to have) _____ a lot of fun."

Reporter: " _____ you _____ (to have) fun right now, too?"

Sue: "Yes, I (to be) _____ , although I (to feel) _____

a bit tired now. At the moment my friends (to wait) _____ for

me. Look, they (to stand) _____ over there.

My mother (to jump) _____ up and down. And Sally

(to shout) _____ my name. I have to go."

Reporter: "Thank you for the interview, Sue. Have a nice day."   14

4

 21 – 17 Punkte
 16 – 11 Punkte
 10 – 0 Punkte
 Gesamt- punktzahl

simple present / present progressive / simple past

Bob's grandfather has got a very old diary which was written by one of his ancestors* more than 300 years ago in London!
For the first time he shows two pages of this diary to Bob.

1 **Put the verbs in the correct tense: simple present, present progressive or simple past.**

September 6, 1666
London

Two days ago a terrible fire (to break out) _____ in a very narrow

street. This (to be) _____ London's second disaster in the last two

years. 68,000 people (to die) _____ from the plague** last year in

1665. The plague (to spread***) _____ through London very quickly

and there (to be) _____ no medicine for the people. When the plague

(to hit) _____ the house of a family the police (to lock) _____

the house. Then they (to paint) _____ a red cross on the front door

and everybody (to know) _____ that the plague (to be) _____

in that house. Every day men with carts**** (to go) _____ through

the streets and (to shout) _____: "Bring out your dead!" They

(to take) _____ the dead bodies away and (to drop) _____

them into a big hole in the ground with thousands of others. And now

London (to burn) _____. Most of the houses in London

(to burn) _____ right now.

There (to be) _____ fires everywhere. Even St. Paul's Cathedral

(to be) _____ on fire. Early last Saturday morning the fire (to start)

_____ in a bakery in Pudding Lane. A policeman (to wake)

_____ Sir Thomas Bloodworth, the Lord Mayor***** of London, but

he (to say) _____ it (to be) _____ nothing and (to go)

_____ back to bed. King Charles II (to tell) _____ the people

yesterday to pull down the houses next to the fire. Nowadays****** we

always (to do) _____ what the king (to say) _____ and so

yesterday a lot of people (to start) _____ to pull down their houses

and (to save) _____ other buildings in London from the fire.

| 28 |

* *ancestor* = Vorfahr, Ahne   ** *the plague* = die Pest   *** *to spread* = sich ausbreiten
**** *cart* = Karren   ***** *Lord Mayor* = (Ober-)Bürgermeister
****** *nowadays* = heutzutage

  28 – 23 **Punkte**  22 – 15 **Punkte**  14 – 0 **Punkte**  **Gesamt-punktzahl**

present perfect

Das *present perfect* wird gebildet aus *have / has* und der 3. Form des Verbs (*past participle*).
Das *present perfect* mit *since* und *for* drückt aus, wie lange ein Zustand oder eine Handlung schon andauert. In Verbindung mit **Zeitpunkten** steht *since*. In Verbindung mit **Zeitspannen** steht *for*, z. B.:
She **hasn't seen** him **since** last Wednesday.
She **hasn't seen** him **for** more than a week.

1 **Fill in "since" or "for" and the correct forms of the present perfect.**

'Hello, my name is Jack Johnson. I'm your tour guide today. I (to live)

_____ in London *for* 16 years and I can tell you a lot of

things about it. I (to be) _____ a tour guide *since* 1990,

that means I have been doing this job _____ quite a long time. We start

our tour at Hyde Park which (to be) _____ famous _____

many years. In 1908 a man stood on a chair on a Sunday morning and

started talking about politics:

_____ then this part of Hyde Park has been

known as "Speaker's Corner".

Now we are driving along Oxford Street. It (to be) _____ a

popular shopping street with a lot of big department stores _____ a long

time. Right in front of you you can see Buckingham Palace. It's a beautiful

building and (to be) _____ the Queen's home _____

she became Queen in 1952. On your right you can see Westminster Abbey.

Many coronations* of kings and queens (to take)

_____ place here _____

about 900 years.

In the distance you can now see the Docklands,

which (to be) _____ a modern

business area with many offices _____ the beginning of 1990.

Many tourists (to visit) _____ the Docklands

_____ then.

Across the River Thames you can see

the Tower of London. In the Tower

you can see the Jewel House which

(to have) _____

a collection of jewels _____ 1661. *Since* that time more and more jewels

have been added**. Near the Tower you find Tower Bridge which was opened

in 1894. Millions of tourists (to take) _____ pictures of this

very famous sight of London _____ then. Now it's the end of our tour.

I hope you (to enjoy) _____ your trip with me

_____ the last two hours. Have a nice day in London.'

22

coronation = Krönung   ** *have been added* = wurden hinzugefügt

    22–18 **Punkte**   17–12 **Punkte**    11–0 **Punkte**    **Gesamt- punktzahl**

Das **Futur mit *will*** drückt Dinge in der Zukunft aus, auf die man keinen Einfluss hat, **Vermutungen über die Zukunft und spontane Handlungen**. Das *will-future* ist die am häufigsten verwendete Futurform im Englischen.
Beispiele:
Vicky will be fourteen next year. I think she will give a party.
Oh well, I will go home now.

Das **Futur mit *going to*** drückt **Absichten und Pläne**, auch begründete Vermutungen für die nahe Zukunft aus.
Beispiele:
I am going to watch TV tonight.
I am going to spend my summer holiday in Spain this year.
Look at those clouds! It's going to rain.

1 Each of the pictures has two corresponding sentences. But only one of them is correct! Look at the pictures and choose the right sentence.
Each sentence has a letter at the end. Write these letters at the bottom of the next page. What word have you written down?

1. a) Perhaps Sarah will go to Scotland or maybe she will go to Sweden. (h)
   b) Perhaps Sarah is going to go to Scotland or maybe she is going to go to Sweden. (t)

2. a) Maybe Hannah will lie on the beach this summer. (o)
   b) Maybe Hannah is going to lie on the beach. (u)

3. a) Mr Pott will paint his house
   this summer. (m)
   b) Mr Pott is going to paint his
   house this summer. (l)

4. a) Lisa is going to visit a museum tomorrow. (i)
   b) Lisa will visit a museum tomorrow. (n)

5. a) Jamie and Ben have just bought a
   new tent because they'll go
   camping this July. (m)
   b) Jamie and Ben have just bought a new
   tent because they're going to go
   camping this July. (d)

6. Josh: My father wants to go on a
   bike tour in June.
   a) I think I'll go with him but I must
   fix my bike first. (a)
   b) I think I'm going to go with him
   but I must fix my bike first. (u)

7. Alan: "What have you got there?"
   a) Lisa: "My plane ticket. I'll visit my grandparents in Canada this summer." (p)
   b) Lisa: "My plane ticket. I'm going to visit my
   grandparents in Canada this summer." (y)

8. Sue: "Where are you going?"
   a) Tina: "I'll book a two-week holiday
   on Majorca. It's so cheap." (f)
   b) Tina: "I'm going to book a two-
   week holiday on Majorca. It's so
   cheap." (s)

___ ___ ___ ___ ___ ___ ___ ___
1   2   3   4   5   6   7   8

| 8 |

27

 ☐

 8–7
Punkte

 6–5
Punkte

 4–0
Punkte

☐ **Gesamt-
punktzahl**

Vermischte Übungen

Hier kannst du überprüfen, was du schon kannst.
Tipp: Wenn du Schwierigkeiten hast, schau auf den in Klammern angegebenen Seiten nach.

1   Fill in the right reflexive pronouns or "each other". (page 10–11)

1. The two friends always helped _____ .

2. The old man talks to _____ .

3. Lisa and Tina always help _____ with their homework.

4. Please help _____ to more cake, Josh and Jamie! | 4 |

★ **2   Modal auxiliaries: Write down the following sentences in the simple past and then in the correct forms of the future. (page 12–13)**

1. You needn't come by bus. _____

    _____

2. I can walk through the park. _____

    _____

3. She mustn't take my bike. _____

    _____ | 6 |

3   Translate the following sentences into English and practise the gerund. (page 14–17)

1. Sally spielt gern Fußball. _____

2. Die Kinder hassen es, einkaufen zu gehen. _____

    _____

Lösungen

1 Wortarten: Adjektiv und Adverb

Seite 4–5

①

adjective	adverb
polite	politely
clear	clearly
comfortable	comfortably
happy	happily
quiet	quietly
quick	quickly
careful	carefully

adjective	adverb
impolite	impolitely
unclear	unclearly
uncomfortable	uncomfortably
unhappy	unhappily
noisy	noisily
slow	slowly
careless	carelessly

②
2. quickly
3. comfortably
4. quietly
5. carefully
6. clearly
7. happily
8. impolitely
9. slowly
10. uncomfortably
11. noisily
12. carelessly
13. unclearly
14. unhappily

Seite 6–7

① 2. Italy, Italian; 3. Germany, German;
4. France, French; 5. Japan, Japanese;
6. Spain, Spanish; 7. Denmark, Danish;
8. Ireland, Irish oder: English

② 2. French trains go faster than Italian trains.
3. The English look after their gardens more carefully than the French.
4. Most French people eat more exquisitely than the English.
5. The Italians relax more easily than the Swiss.
6. Japanese people speak more quietly than Italians.
7. Germans talk more slowly than the French.

2 Wortarten: Pronomen und Mengenangaben

Seite 8–9

① 2. yours, 3. hers, yours, Yours, hers,
4. theirs, 5. theirs, 6. ours, 7. yours,
8. mine, 9. yours, 10. mine, 11. yours,
12. mine, 13. ours, ours

Seite 10–11

① myself, yourself, himself, ourselves,
myself, yourselves, myself, yourselves,
ourselves, yourself, myself

② ★ 2. Cats clean themselves every day.
3. Ben and Josh talked to each other yesterday.
4. Usually I repair my bike myself.
5. Jamie and Sarah help each other with their homework every day.
6. Hannah looks at herself in the mirror every morning.

29

3 Wortarten: Das Verb

Seite 12–13

1 Jim had to take the number 8. He had to get off at Colin's Chip Shop. He <u>was not allowed to get off</u> at the cinema because then he <u>had to walk</u> much further. From Colin's Chip Shop he only <u>had to walk</u> for about five minutes. He <u>could see</u> the back of Alan's house from the bus stop but he <u>was not allowed to climb</u> over the garden fence. He <u>didn't have to walk</u> along the road. He <u>could walk</u> through the park. If he <u>could not find</u> his way, he <u>could phone</u> Alan and Alan <u>could collect</u> him from the phone box. He <u>didn't have to buy</u> a return ticket.

2 ★ 2. will have to, 3. will have to walk, 4. will be able, 5. won't have to, 6. will be able

Seite 14–15

1 3. Tina likes going to the cinema.
4. Sue loves/enjoys going swimming.
5. Does Jim like washing the dishes? No, he dislikes washing the dishes.
6. Bob likes playing the piano.
7. Sue hates riding horses.
8. Does Bob love/enjoy reading books? Yes, he loves/enjoys reading books.
9. Tina loves/enjoys playing computer games.
10. Does Sue like going to pop concerts? Yes, she likes going to pop concerts.
11. Bob dislikes going shopping.
12. Sue dislikes learning vocabulary.

2 Jim likes playing tennis.
Tina likes watching TV.
Bob dislikes going to school.
Sue likes eating pizza.

Seite 16–17

1 2. Playing party games is stupid.
3. Moving the furniture is necessary as we need room to dance.
4. Making a cake is unnecessary as Mum is baking one.
5. Organizing music is necessary as I haven't got enough CDs.
6. Buying candles is necessary as they make great light.

2 1. Bob is tired of cycling.
2. Mrs Pott is very interested in buying clothes.
3. Jamie is crazy about climbing mountains.
4. Some dogs aren't afraid of jumping into the water.
5. Hannah is good at writing stories.
6. Josh is bad at playing chess.
7. Mr Brown is famous for running 100 metres in 11 seconds.

Seite 18–19

1 2. The guide tells <u>the tourists</u> <u>the history of the castle</u>.
3. I will send <u>all my friends</u> <u>postcards</u>.
4. The waiter will bring <u>a cup of tea</u> for <u>us</u>.
5. "Give your <u>camera</u> to <u>me</u>!"
6. The man offered <u>the tourists</u> <u>photos of the ghost</u>.
7. In the end he sold <u>more than 20 photos</u> to <u>the tourists</u>.

2 1. "Give Jim the map of the town!"
2. My father tells the group of visitors the story of the castle.
3. Our teacher wanted to buy the class tickets for a sightseeing tour.
4. The cook made them soup.
5. My mother asked me to bring her a T-shirt from Wales.

3 ★ 1. The teacher gave the pupils texts on Wales. Oder: The teacher gave texts on Wales to the pupils.
2. I sent two postcards to my friends. Oder: I sent my friends two postcards.
3. The tourists bought their friends a lot of souvenirs. Oder: The tourists bought a lot of souvenirs for their friends.
4. The guide showed the tourists the way. Oder: The guide showed the way to the tourists.
5. My mother bought (has bought) James a T-shirt. Oder: My mother bought (has bought) a T-shirt for James.
6. Ben wrote three emails to his sister. Oder: Ben wrote his sister three emails.
7. "Please bring me a cup of coffee."

4 Die Zeitformen des Verbs

Seite 20 – 21

1 gets up, goes, does, isn't, swim, trains, run

2 do, have, don't do, go, swims, runs, have, Are ... having, am, am feeling, are waiting, are standing, is jumping, is shouting

Seite 22 – 23

1 broke out, was, died, spread, was, hit, locked, painted, knew, was, went, shouted, took, dropped, is burning, are burning, are, is, started, woke, said, was, went, told, do, says, started, saved

Seite 24 – 25

1 have lived, have been, for, has been, for, since, has been, for, has been, since, have taken, for, have been, since, have visited, since, has had, since, have taken, since, have enjoyed, for

Seite 26 – 27

1 1. a), 2. a), 3. b), 4. a),
5. b), 6. a), 7 b), 8. b)
Lösungswort: holidays

Seite 28 / 37

1 1. each other, 2. himself,
3. each other, 4. yourselves

2 ★ 1. You didn't have to come by bus. You will not (won't) have to come by bus.
2. I was able to walk through the park. I will be able to walk through the park. Oder: I was allowed to walk through the park. I will be allowed to walk through the park.
3. She wasn't allowed to take my bike. She will not (won't) be allowed to take my bike.

③
1. Sally likes playing football.
2. The children hate going shopping.
3. Ben loves playing computer games.
4. Does Josh like washing the dishes?
   Oder: Does Josh like doing the washing-up?

④
1. Mrs Brown often goes to London at the weekend.
2. Every Monday the children play street-ball.
3. Look! The dog is running in the garden.
4. Mr Pott is sitting in the living room and watching TV right now.

⑤ for, since, since, for, since

Seite 38 – 39

①
2. "What's your hobby, Lisa and Tina?"
   "We play table tennis."
   "How long have you been playing table tennis?"
   "We have (We've) been playing table tennis for two weeks."
3. "I play basketball, too."
   "How long have you been playing basketball?"
   "I have (I've) been playing basketball since last summer."
4. "I read books, too."
   "How long have you been reading books?"
   "I have (I've) been reading books for five years."

②
2. Jim has been riding his bike since his 10th birthday.
3. Alan has been climbing mountains since the summer of 2009.
4. Sue has been going swimming for three years.
5. Jim has been taking photos since Christmas.
6. Sue has been playing the guitar for more than two years.
7. Alan has been collecting comics for less than four years.

Seite 40 – 41

①
3. Jim Harvey has had a bad accident on his bicycle.
4. Sue has been playing the guitar since breakfast.
5. Ben has been reading for a very long time.
6. Alan hasn't decided yet where to spend his holiday.
7. Josh has used his knife to open a tin.
8. Lisa has been trying to call Tina for one hour.

Seite 42 – 43

①
2. When I smelled the fire I was reading a book.
3. I was talking to a friend on the phone when the fire broke out.
4. I was playing the guitar when I heard somebody shout "Fire!".
5. We were having dinner.
6. I was repairing my CD player.
7. When we heard the fire alarm we were playing cards.

2 1. Ms Conrad was reading a book.
2. No, the Taylors were having dinner.
3. Elissa was playing the guitar.
4. No, Robert was repairing his CD player.
5. Mr and Mrs Spencer were playing cards.
6. Jason and Tina were watching TV.

Seite 44 – 45

1 1. King Edward of England died without a son.
2. He himself was the son of a Norman princess.
3. Years ago he had promised the crown to William, Duke of Normandy.
4. But now the English didn't want a Norman king.
5. They chose Harold as King of England.
Lösungswort: battle

2 ★ 1. were waiting, landed
2. were marching, met, won, died
3. were hurrying, fell, was, got up, looked, shouted
4. were marching, were carrying, attacked, were, fought
5. was getting, spread, was, was
6. became

Seite 46 – 47

1 The music is composed by Mr Thompson.
The bands are interviewed by Ms Mitchell.
The pop stars are invited by Mr Caldwell.
The studio is decorated with posters by Ms Fulton.
The songs are recorded in a special room by Ms Hart.
The songs are played on the radio by Mr Hull.
The pop stars' contracts are signed by Mr Watson.
The managers of the bands are met by Ms Black.
The doors are kept shut during recording by Mr Richard.

2 2. Is the studio decorated with posters by Ms Hart?
3. Are the pop stars' contracts signed by Mr Scott?

1 Yesterday gold was found in California.
The San Francisco Marathon was run by 4,281 people.
Seven new motorways were built in 2012.
A truck driver was stopped by the police.
A thief was seen by a clever neighbour.
Five men were injured in a gas explosion.
Three museums were newly decorated for the expo.
Everything was repaired after the power cut.
Graffiti were written on walls by an unknown person.
A boy was given a dangerous injection before an operation.
The latest rock CD was sold out yesterday.
152 cars were destroyed by a thunderstorm.
The train passengers were interviewed after the accident.
A woman was bitten by a fox in her own home.

1 At 7.30 a.m. Jamie's temperature is taken.
At 8.15 a.m. new bandages are put around his knee and elbow.
At 12.00 Jamie is fed by the nurse.
At 3.00 p.m. Jamie is given an injection by the doctor.

2 Jamie was taken to the x-ray room. He was given his medicine at 5 o'clock.
His wounds were cleaned. His patient's report was written at once. His bed was made twice. The bandages on his elbow and knee were changed. His arm was put in plaster. He was helped with dinner. He was told to drink at least two litres of water.

5 Der Satz

1 2. If you want to start a new line, press this key.
3. If you want to write in capital letters, press this key.
4. If you press this key, you will take the cursor down a line.
5. If you press the key "Pos 1", you will go to the beginning of a line.
6. If you press the key "Ende", you will go to the end of a line. Oder: If you want to go to the end of a line, press this key. Oder: Press this key if you want to go to the end of a line.
7. If you want to go back and delete the last letter, press this key. Oder: Press this key if you want to go back and delete the last letter. Oder: If you press this key, you will go back and delete the last letter.
8. If you want to delete the following letter, press this key. Oder: Press this key if you want to delete the following letter. Oder: If you press this key, you will delete the following letter.

2 2. If it rains, the children will play in the living room in the evening.
3. If Ben buys a new basketball, he can play with his friends tomorrow.
4. If you have toothache, go to the dentist!

Seite 54 – 55

1 ★ 2. music, 3. comes, 4. forks, 5. next,
6. Thursday
Lösungswort: ticket

2 would go, went, would earn, earned,
would/could buy, went, would/could see,
got, would be, talked, would come

3 1. If the sun shone, we would go for
a walk.
2. If it rained, the children would/could
play in the living room.
3. If Ben bought a new basketball,
he could play with his friends.

Seite 56 – 57

1/**2**
1. If you spend your holiday in the
country, you will see a lot of cows and
sheep in the fields. (T)
2. If you want to go shopping, you will
find more big department stores in
a town. (R)
3. If you lived in a town, you wouldn't
have to travel so far to school. (A)
4. If I had to buy a new dress, I would
look for one in the new shop opposite
the station. (F)
5. If I lived in a house in the country,
I would enjoy the good air there. (F)
6. If the Coopers moved to the country-
side, their children would miss their
old friends, but they could play in
the fields. (I)
7. If more people go to town by car, the
car parks will be very crowded. (C)
Lösungswort: traffic

3 ★ 2. would go, would pay, would sell,
3. stay, 4. will not have, 5. moves,
6. goes, will be, will miss, 7. would earn,
8. will have, 9. would miss

Seite 58 – 59

1

who	which
the dancer who	the CD which
the film star who	the house which
the people who	the banana which
the teacher who	the ticket which
the manager who	the music which
the singer who	the story which
the girls who	the records which
the dentist who	the book which

2 who (R), who (E), who (A), which (T),
which (M), who (U), which (S), who (I),
which (C)
Lösungswörter: great music

3 1. who, 2. who, 3. which,
4. which, 5. who, 6. who

Seite 60 – 61

1 2. Deanna is in class 3 C, which is a very
noisy class. Oder: ..., which is very
noisy.
3. In her class, there are 29 pupils, who all
come from different parts of the city.
Oder: There are 29 pupils in her class,
who ...
4. Mr Green, who is her new English
teacher, is her favourite teacher.
Oder: Mr Green, who is her favourite
teacher, is her new English teacher.
5. The school's gym, which is in Dover
Street, is quite old. Oder: The school's
gym, which is quite old, is in Dover
Street.
6. Deanna has got a new timetable, which
is different from her old one.
7. There's physical education, which
Deanna hates, on Monday. Oder: On
Monday, there's physical education,
which Deanna hates.

8. Her new friend Jennifer, who sits next to her, is always late for school. Oder: Her new friend Jennifer, who is always late for school, sits next to her.

9. Deanna's classroom, which is on the third floor, is room number 318. Oder: Deanna's classroom, which is room number 318, is on the third floor. Oder: Deanna's classroom is room number 318, which is on the third floor.

10. Deanna likes Alan, who is a new boy in her class, very much.

11. Mr Petit, who is from France, is Deanna's new French teacher. Oder: Mr Petit, who is Deanna's new French teacher, is from France.

12. Deanna likes her biology teacher, who is the youngest teacher at the school.

13. Deanna's classroom, which is on the third floor, has a nice view. Oder: Deanna's classroom, which has a nice view, is on the third floor.

Seite 62 – 63

①
1. Tina was working in her room when suddenly the light went out.
2. She was waiting in her room when the telephone rang.
3. Suddenly the light went on again while she was talking/speaking to her friend.
4. Tina's parents came home while Tina was playing a computer game.

② ★
1. The guests were invited by Bob last week.
2. Bob's father wrote the invitations on the computer.
3. All the food was made by Bob and his mother.
4. At 10 o'clock the guests are taken home by Bob's father. Oder: The guests are taken home by Bob's father at 10 o'clock. Oder: The guests are taken home at 10 o'clock by Bob's father.

③
1. would get, 2. take, 3. could join, 4. had, 5. felt, 6. would win

④
which, who, who, which, which, who, which, who

3. Ben liebt es, Computerspiele zu spielen. _____

_____

4. Spült Josh gerne? _____ | 4 |

4 **Make sentences. Use the correct forms of the simple present OR the present progressive. (page 20–23)**

1. Mrs Brown / often / to go / to London / at the weekend

_____

2. Every Monday / the children / to play / streetball

_____

3. Look! / The dog / to run / in the garden

_____

4. Mr Pott / to sit / in living room / and / to watch TV / right now

_____ | 4 |

5 **Fill in "since" or "for". (page 24–25)**

Mr Parker has been a teacher _____ ten years. He has been the class

teacher of class 7A _____ 2002. The pupils have been learning French

with Mr Parker _____ he came to Woodland High School.

He wants to take his French class to Paris this spring. He has been planning

this trip _____ a long time. He has been cycling to school _____

last summer. | 5 | **37**

present perfect progressive

Das **present perfect progressive** wird gebildet aus einer Form von *to have* + *been* + *-ing*-Form (= Partizip Präsens).
Das *present perfect progressive* drückt besonders **Tätigkeiten** (wie *to do, to make, to read*) und **Vorgänge** (wie *to rain, to grow*) aus, die schon eine **Zeit lang andauern**, z. B.:
She **has been running** for over two hours now and she still has 6 miles to go.
I**'ve been reading** for two hours and I haven't finished yet.

Achtung: Verben, die Zustände beschreiben (wie *to be, to like, to know*), werden nicht im *present perfect progressive* verwendet.

1 **Janet is a reporter. Right now she is asking Bob, Lisa and Tina about their hobbies. Look at the words in brackets and complete the dialogues.**

1. Janet: (What?) *"What's your hobby, Bob?"*

   Bob: (sammelt Actionfiguren) *"I collect action figures."*

   Janet: (How long?) *"How long have you been collecting action figures?"*

   Bob: (2010) *"I've been collecting action figures since 2010."*

2. Janet: (What?) _____

   Lisa and Tina: (spielen Tischtennis) *We* _____

   Janet: (How long?) _____

   Lisa and Tina: (2 weeks) _____

   _____

3. Lisa: (spielt auch Basketball) _____

   Janet: (How long?) _____

   Lisa: (last summer) _____

4. Bob: (liest auch Bücher) _____

Janet: (How long?) _____

Bob: (5 years) _____ | 10 |

2 Janet also spoke to Alan, Jim and Sue about their hobbies. Look at Janet's notes and complete the sentences.

name	hobby	How long?
Alan	plays the piano	6 years
Jim	rides his bike	his 10th birthday
Alan	climbs mountains	the summer of 2009
Sue	goes swimming	3 years
Jim	takes photos	Christmas
Sue	plays the guitar	more than 2 years
Alan	collects comics	less than 4 years

1. Alan *has been playing the piano for six years.*

2. Jim _____

3. Alan _____

4. Sue _____

5. Jim _____

6. Sue _____

7. Alan _____ | 6 |

present perfect /
present perfect progressive

Ein paar Tipps zur **Unterscheidung von *present perfect* und
present perfect progressive:**

present perfect	*present perfect progressive*
wird meist ohne eine genauere Zeitangabe gebraucht	kommt fast immer mit einer Zeitangabe vor, z. B.: *for two hours, since 2011, for a long time, since 5 o'clock*
beschreibt Zustände und Handlungen, die in der Vergangenheit begonnen haben und jetzt noch Auswirkung haben oder gerade erst abgeschlossen wurden	beschreibt schon länger und jetzt immer noch andauernde Handlungen
wird sehr oft nach folgenden Ausdrücken gebraucht: *(not) yet, already, so far, just* (= gerade eben), *up to now*	Verben, die Zustände, Meinungen und Bewertungen beschreiben, bilden das *present perfect progressive* normalerweise nicht, z. B.: *to be, to exist, to have, to smell, to need, to agree, to believe, to think, to like, to dislike, to love, to hate*

1 **Look at the pictures and complete the corresponding sentences using the present perfect OR the present perfect progressive.
Don't forget "since" or "for" where necessary!**

1. Mr Brown / a new car / to buy

   Mr Brown has bought a new car.

2. to play / three hours / tennis / Tina

   Tina has been playing tennis for three hours.

3. to have / a bad accident / Jim Harvey / on his bicycle

_____

4. the guitar / Sue / to play / breakfast

_____

5. Ben / to read / for a very long time_____

_____ And he is still reading now!

6. not to decide / Alan / yet / where to spend his holiday

_____

7. to use / Josh / his knife / to open a tin*

_____

8. Lisa / to try / to call Tina / one hour

_____

6

* *tin* = Dose

  6 – 5
Punkte    4 – 3
Punkte    2 – 0
Punkte    **Gesamt-punktzahl**

past progressive

Das *past progressive* drückt eine **Handlung** aus, die zu einer bestimmten Zeit **in der Vergangenheit** im Gange, also **noch nicht beendet** war, z. B.:
I was reading in my room yesterday at 4 o'clock.

Oft beschreibt das *past progressive* auch eine Handlung in der Vergangenheit, die im Gange war, während gleichzeitig (auch in der Vergangenheit) noch etwas anderes passierte, z. B.:
I was reading when the telephone rang.

A fire in Woodland Street

There was a fire in 22 Woodland Street two days ago. Now the policemen together with the firemen want to find out who started the fire and where. They want to know what everybody in the house was doing when the fire broke out. Here is a list of what everybody was doing. Look at the list.

people	what they were doing
Jason and Tina	watch TV
Mr Johnson	talk to a friend on the phone
Elissa	play the guitar
Ms Conrad	read a book
Robert	repair his CD player
Mr and Mrs Spencer	play cards
The Taylors	have dinner

1 **Now complete these sentences using the past progressive.**

1. Jason and Tina: *We were watching TV when we heard the fire alarm*.

2. Ms Conrad: *When I smelled the fire* _____ .

3. Mr Johnson: _____

_____ *when the fire broke out*.

4. Elissa: _____ *when I heard*

somebody shout "Fire!".

5. The Taylors: *We* _____ .

6. Robert: _____ *my CD player*.

7. Mr and Mrs Spencer: *When we heard the fire alarm* _____

_____ . `6`

---

② Police inspector Smith has lost the list. So he must ask officer Sniff for help. Write down Sniff's answers.

1. Smith: What was Ms Conrad doing?

   Sniff: _____

2. Smith: Were the Taylors having lunch?

   Sniff: _____

3. Smith: What was Elissa doing?

   Sniff: _____

4. Smith: Was Robert reading a book?

   Sniff: _____

5. Smith: Who was playing cards?

   Sniff: _____

6. Smith: What were Jason and Tina doing?

   Sniff: _____ `6`

 12 – 10 **Punkte**
 9 – 7 **Punkte**
 6 – 0 **Punkte**
 **Gesamt-punktzahl**

simple past / past progressive

1 **Match the parts of the sentences. Fill in the letters for the solution word.**

1. King Edward of England	Harold as King of England. (L)
2. He himself was	the crown to William, Duke of Normandy. (T)
3. Years ago he had promised*	died without a son. (B)
4. But now the English	also wanted to become King of England. (E)
5. They chose	didn't want a Norman king. (T)
6. The King of Norway	the son of a Norman princess. (A)

* to promise = versprechen

After a long fight the Normans won the ____ ____ ____ ____ ____ _E_
of Hastings.   1   2   3   4   5   6 | 5 |

★ 2 **A historical story: Fill in the right forms of the simple past or the past progressive.**

Summer 1066

1. While William and his men (to wait) _____

   for good winds to sail to England, the King of Norway (to land)

   _____ in the north of England.

2. Harold of England and his men (to march)

   _____ north when they

   suddenly (to meet) _____ the

   King of Norway in the north of England. Harold

   (to win) _____ the hard battles

   but a lot of soldiers (to die)_____.

September 1066

3. Lots of Norman soldiers (to hurry) _____ up the

    English beach when one of them suddenly (to fall) _____

    on the sand. It (to be) _____ William. He (to get up)

    _____, (to look) _____ at his

    men and (to shout) _____:

    "Look, England is in my hands already."

October 1066

4. King Harold and 8,000 soldiers (to march)

    _____ to the south of England and they (to carry)

    _____ a lot of things with them, when one morning the

    Normans (to attack) _____ them. They (to be)

    _____ faster on their horses and they (to fight)

    _____ with bows and arrows.

5. It (to get) _____ dark when suddenly somebody (to spread)

    _____ the news that King Harold (to be) _____

    dead. The battle (to be) _____ over.

Christmas 1066

6. William (to become) _____ the first Norman king on

    the English throne on Christmas Day in 1066.

| 22 |

    22 – 19 Punkte    18 – 12 Punkte    11 – 0 Punkte       Gesamt-punktzahl

Das **Aktiv** drückt aus, **wer etwas tut**. Das Subjekt des Aktivsatzes vollzieht eine Handlung, z. B.:

Policemen	*write*	*reports.*
(subject)	*(verb)*	*(object)*
Polizisten	schreiben	Berichte.

Das **Passiv** drückt aus, **womit etwas geschieht**. An dem Subjekt des Passivsatzes wird eine Handlung vollzogen.

Das Passiv wird gebildet mit einer Form von *to be* und dem Partizip Perfekt (*past participle*), z. B.:

Reports	**are written**	*by policemen.*	
(subject)	*(verb)*	*(object)*	
Berichte	werden	von Polizisten	geschrieben.

A lot of people work in the recording studio. Read what their jobs are:

Mr Scott: I write the lyrics* for the songs.
Mr Thompson: I compose the music.
Ms Mitchell: I interview the bands.
Mr Caldwell: I invite the pop stars.
Ms Fulton: I decorate the studio with posters.
Ms Hart: I record the songs in a special room.
Mr Hull: I play the songs on the radio.
Mr Watson: I sign the pop stars' contracts.**
Ms Black: I meet the managers of the bands.
Mr Richard: I must keep the doors shut during recording.

* *lyrics* = Liedtexte   ** *contract* = Vertrag

1 **What is done by what person in the recording studio? Write down the sentences in the passive simple present.**

The lyrics for the songs are written by Mr Scott.

The music is _____

_____

_____

_____

_____

_____

_____

_____

_____

| 9 |

_____

2 **Mr Brown is new in the studio. He asks a lot of questions. Look at the answers and write down Mr Brown's questions.**

1. *Are the bands interviewed by Mr Hull?*

   No, the bands are not interviewed by Mr Hull.

2. _____

   No, the studio isn't decorated with posters by Ms Hart.

3. _____

   No, the pop stars' contracts are not signed by Mr Scott.

| 2 |

47

passive simple past

Das *simple past* des Passivs wird gebildet, indem die entsprechende Form von *to be* in das *simple past* gesetzt wird, z. B.:
passive simple present: *The report **is** written by a policeman.*
passive simple past: *The report **was** written by a policeman.*

San Francisco Marathon run by 4,281 people

Truck driver stopped by police

Seven new motorways built in 2012

Thief seen by clever neighbour

Five men injured in gas explosion

Three museums newly decorated for the expo

Gold found in California

Everything repaired after the power cut

Graffiti written on walls by unknown person

Boy given dangerous injection before operation

Latest rock CD sold out yesterday

152 cars destroyed by thunderstorm

Train passengers interviewed after accident

Woman bitten by fox in her own home

1 Imagine, you are the newsreader on TV. Before you read out the news write down the complete news in the passive simple past. Add the definite or indefinite article where necessary.

Good evening.
Here is the latest news.

Yesterday gold was found in _____

_____

_____

_____

_____

_____

_____

_____

_____

_____

_____

_____ | 13 |

 **13 – 10 Punkte**   **9 – 7 Punkte**   **6 – 0 Punkte**    **Gesamtpunktzahl**

passive simple present /
passive simple past

Jamie had an accident with his bike. He must stay in hospital for one day.

1 **Write down what happens to Jamie in hospital. Use the passive simple present.**

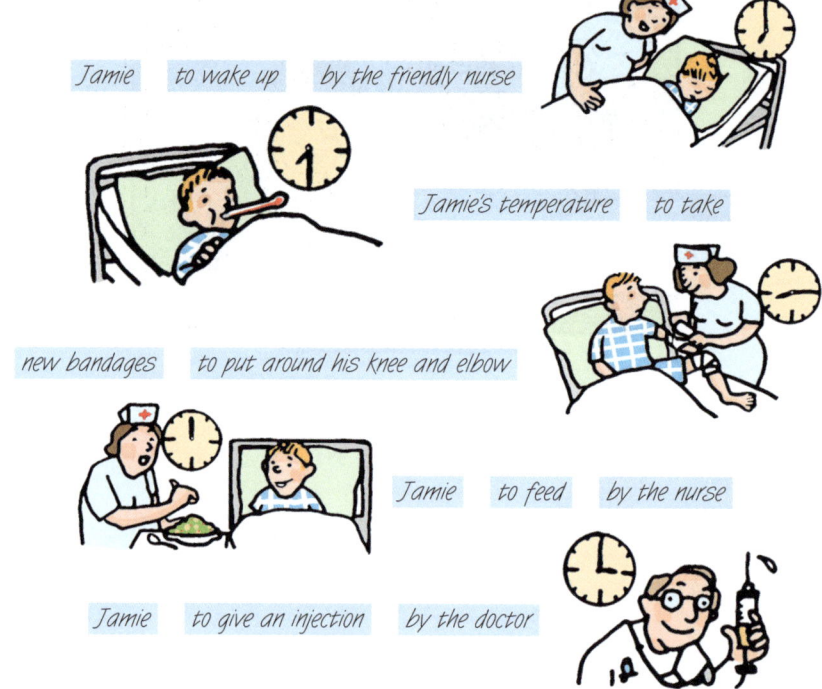

Jamie   to wake up   by the friendly nurse

Jamie's temperature   to take

new bandages   to put around his knee and elbow

Jamie   to feed   by the nurse

Jamie   to give an injection   by the doctor

At 7.00 a.m. Jamie is woken up by the friendly nurse.

At 7.30 a.m. _____

_____

_____

_____

_____

4

Yesterday morning the doctor told the nurse what to do with Jamie.

Doctor: "Give Jamie Brown an injection.
Take him to the x-ray* room.
Give Jamie Brown his medicine
at 5 o'clock. Clean his wounds**.
Write Jamie's patient's report at once.
Make his bed twice a day. Change
the bandages on his elbow and knee.
Put Jamie Brown's arm in plaster.
Help him with dinner. Tell him to
drink at least two litres of water."

* *x-ray* = Röntgen   ** *wound* = Wunde

2 **Write down what was done yesterday.**

Jamie was given an injection.

_____

_____

_____

_____

_____

_____

_____

_____

_____

_____

| 9 |

51

Bedingungssätze:
if-Sätze im simple present

Bedingungssätze (*conditional sentences*) bestehen aus zwei Teilen: dem *if*-Satz (*if-clause*, Nebensatz mit *if*) und dem Hauptsatz (*main clause*). Der Nebensatz mit *if* drückt eine Bedingung aus. Wenn in dem ***if*-Satz** das ***simple present*** steht, ist die **Erfüllung** dieser Bedingung **möglich oder sogar wahrscheinlich**, z. B.: *If you drop the glass, it will break.*

Wenn in dem *if*-Satz das *simple present* steht, muss im Hauptsatz entweder ein Imperativ (III) oder das *will-future* (II) oder ein anderes Hilfsverb mit einem Infinitiv (I) stehen, z. B.:

if-clause	*main clause*
I: *If Bob gets a new bike,*	*he can go to school by bike.*
II: *If the weather is fine,*	*we will go for a walk.*
III: *If it rains,*	*take an umbrella with you.*

Tina's mum explains some of the most important computer keys*.

* key = (hier:) Taste

1 **Complete Tina's mother's sentences. Use the following phrases.**

~~to take the cursor down a line~~   to go to the end of a line   ~~to make a space*~~

to delete the following letter   to write in capital letters**   to start a new line

to go to the beginning of a line   to go back and delete the last letter

* space = (hier:) Leerzeichen zwischen zwei Wörtern   ** capital letter = Großbuchstabe

1. If you press this key, you *will make a space*.

2. If you want to _____, press this key.

3. If _____, press this key.

4. _____, you will *take the cursor down a line.*

5. If you press the key "Pos 1", _____

   _____

6. _____

   _____

7. _____

   _____

8. _____

   _____

7

2 **Write down conditional sentences using the words given.**

1. the sun / to shine / we / to go / for a walk / after lunch

   If the sun shines, we will go for a walk after lunch.

2. to rain / the children / to play / in the living room / in the evening

   _____

3. Ben / to buy / a new basketball / he / to play / with his friends / tomorrow

   _____

4. you / to have / toothache / to go / the dentist

   _____!

   3

  10 – 9 Punkte  8 – 6 Punkte  5 – 0 Punkte   Gesamt-punktzahl

Bedingungssätze:
if-Sätze im simple past

Wenn der *if*-Satz im *simple past* steht, dann hält man die **Erfüllung** der Bedingung für **eher unwahrscheinlich**. Der Hauptsatz drückt aus, was geschehen könnte oder würde, wenn die Bedingung doch noch erfüllt würde, z. B.: *If I found 2 million pounds, I would buy a plane.*

Wenn in dem *if*-Satz das *simple past* steht, muss im Hauptsatz *would / could / might* mit einem Infinitiv stehen, z. B.:

if-clause	main clause
If the weather was fine,	we would go for a walk.
If Bob got a new bike,	he might go to school by bike.

★ ❶ **Complete the following sentences. If you do it correctly you will be able to write the solution word with six letters.**

1. If you liked something very much, it would be your _f a v o u r i t e_.

   (take letter 8 as the first letter of the solution word)

2. If you played the piano, the guitar or some other instrument, you might make __ __ __ __ __ . (take letter 4 as the second letter of the solution word)

3. He came to town yesterday. He __ __ __ __ __ to town every Monday. (take the first letter)

4. We could eat our meal if the waiter brought knifes, spoons and __ __ __ __ __ . (take letter 4)

5. If you had 1, 2, 3, 4, the __ __ __ __ number would be 5. (take letter 2)

6. __ __ __ __ __ __ __ __ is the fourth day of the week. (take the first letter as the last letter of the solution word)

   If you had enough money, you could buy a _t_ __ __ __ __ __ .

5

Sue has a lot of dreams and wishes.
But she is ill and must stay in bed.
So her wishes cannot
come true!

2 **Fill in the correct tense of the verb.**

If I (not to be) _wasn't_ ill, I (to go) _____ shopping for old

Ms Smith. If I (to go) _____ shopping for Ms Smith, I (to earn)

_____ some money. If I (to earn) _____

some money, I (to buy) _____ a ticket for the pop concert

next month. If I (to go) _____ to the concert, I (to see)

_____ my favourite pop group, "The Wonders". If I (to get)

_____ a fan postcard of "The Wonders", I (to be) _____

very happy. If one of the band members (to talk) _____ to me,

a dream (to come) _____ true.

| 11 |

5

3 **Write down conditional sentences in the simple past.**

1. the sun / to shine / we / to go / for a walk

   If the sun shone, _____

2. to rain / the children / to play / in the living room

   _____

3. Ben / to buy / a new basketball / he / to play / with his friends

   _____   _____

| 3 |

55

Bedingungssätze: simple present / simple past

This is a tricky game! You have to do two things:

1 Take highlighters in different colours and match each *if*-clause from the left with a main clause from the right. With the crossed letters you can make up the missing word in the sentence below.

6

2 Write down the given verb in the correct tense in the *if*-clause. If you can't remember when to use simple present and simple past in an *if*-clause, look at pages 52 and 54 again.

5

1. If you (to spend) *spend* your holiday in the country

2. If you (to want) _____ to go shopping

3. If you (to live) _____ in a town

4. If I (to have to) _____ buy a new dress

5. If I (to live) *lived* in a house in the country

6. If the Coopers (to move) _____ to the country-side

7. If more people (to go) _____ to town by car

their children would miss their old friends, but they could play in the fields.

you wouldn't have to travel so far to school.

you will see a lot of cows and sheep in the fields.

the car parks will be very crowded.

you will find more big department stores in a town.

I would look for one in the new shop opposite the station.

I would enjoy the good air there.

The ____ _R_ ____ ____ ____ ____ in a town can be very heavy.
    1 2 3 4 5 6 7

Deanna's father, Mr Mitchell, has got a new job in a big town. So the Mitchells are thinking about moving from the countryside into town.

★ **3** **Complete the following conditional sentences.**

1. If they didn't move, it (to take) _would take_ Mr Mitchell one and half hours to get to work.

2. If they stayed in the country, he (to go) _____ 60 miles to work every day, he (to pay) _____ a lot of money for petrol and he (to sell) _____ his slow old car soon.

3. If the Mitchells (to stay) _____ in their old house, Mr Mitchell will be on the road for a long time every day.

4. If he has to drive for hours each day, he (not to have) _____ enough time for his hobbies.

5. If the family (to move) _____ to town, Deanna (to have to change) _will have to change_ school.

6. If she (to go) _____ to a new school, it (to be) _____ difficult for her to find new friends and she (to miss) _____ her old friends.

7. If Mrs Mitchell looked for a new job in town, she (to earn) _____ more money.

8. If she stops working, she (to have) _____ more time for her hobbies.

9. If the Mitchells gave up their house in the country, they (to miss) _____ their big garden and all the fresh air.

5

| 12 |

57

Bestimmende Relativsätze

Nebensätze, die ein vorausgehendes Nomen genauer bestimmen, heißen **bestimmende Relativsätze** (*defining relative clauses*). Sie sind **für das Verständnis des Satzes notwendig** und können nicht weggelassen werden. Sie werden durch die Relativpronomen *who, which* oder *that* eingeleitet und stehen **nicht in Kommas**.
Who wird für **Personen** verwendet, z. B.:
The girl who bought that bike is my sister.
The boys who won the race are my brothers.

Which wird für **Dinge** verwendet, ebenfalls im Singular und im Plural, z. B.:
This is the photo which my grandfather gave me yesterday.

That wird für **Personen und Dinge** im Singular und im Plural verwendet, z. B.:
The girl that is crying is Sarah.
The films that I like best are all action films.

1 Put these words in the correct column of the table and write down the correct relative pronoun. Use only "who" or "which".

~~CD~~   ~~dancer~~   film star   house   people   banana   teacher   ticket

manager   music   singer   story   records   girls   dentist   book

who	which
the dancer who	the CD which

14

2 **Underline the correct word. Write the letter behind that word in the space below.**

There is a new disco in our town who (H) / which (G) is very good. All the people who (R) / which (E) go there have a great time. It was my friend Susan who (E) / which (A) asked me to go there next Saturday. She knows the young woman who (A) / which (T) works as a DJ there. I hope this woman will play music who (S) / which (T) I like. In the last disco who (C) / which (M) I went to the DJ played awful music. All the people who (U) / which (O) I talked to there told me they would never go to that disco again.

On Saturday, I will bring along the CD by the 'Humblebums' who (T) / which (S) I bought last week. I will ask the DJ to play it. The young man who (I) / which (E) sold the CD to me really knew what he was talking about. I cannot tell who (M) / which (C) song on the CD I like best – they are all fantastic.

_G_ ____ ____ ____ ____   ____ ____ ____ ____ ____ | 9 |

5

3 **Fill in "who" or "which".**

1. That lady over there was the woman _____ taught me English.

2. It was my brother _____ painted that picture over there.

3. My father gave me a present _____ he bought in Canada.

4. The subject _____ I like best is English.

5. The runner _____ won the marathon was very happy afterwards.

6. The girl _____ you saw at the disco yesterday is my cousin.

| 6 |

    29 – 24 Punkte  23 – 16 Punkte  15 – 0 Punkte  Gesamt-punktzahl

Nicht bestimmende Relativsätze

Nicht bestimmende Relativsätze (*non-defining relative clauses*) sind Relativsätze, die **nicht notwendig zum Verständnis des Satzes** sind. Man könnte sie weglassen und würde den Satz doch verstehen. *Non-defining relative clauses* werden **durch Kommas** vom Hauptsatz abgetrennt, z. B.:
*John, **who** lives next door to me, is very friendly.*
*I always spend my holidays in Cornwall, **which** is a very nice part of England.*

Auch hier gilt: **who** für Personen, **which** für Dinge.

Here are some sentences about Deanna's new school.

1. Ms Oldfield is her new headteacher. She is very strict.
2. Deanna is in class 3C. It's a very noisy class.
3. In her class, there are 29 pupils. They all come from different parts of the city.
4. Mr Green is her favourite teacher. He is her new English teacher.
5. The school's gym is quite old. It's in Dover Street.
6. Deanna has got a new timetable. It's different from her old one.
7. There's physical education* on Monday. Deanna hates it.
8. Her new friend Jennifer is always late for school. Jennifer sits next to her.
9. Deanna's classroom is room number 318. It's on the third floor.
10. Deanna likes Alan very much. He is a new boy in her class.
11. Mr Petit is Deanna's new French teacher. He is from France.
12. Deanna likes her biology teacher. She is the youngest teacher at the school.
13. Deanna's classroom has a nice view. It is on the third floor.

* *physical education* = Sport (als Schulfach)

1 **Rewrite the sentences about Deanna's school. Use non-defining relative clauses.**

1. *Ms Oldfield, who is very strict, is Deanna's new headteacher.*

2. *Deanna is in class 3 C,* _____

3. _____

_____

4. _____

_____

5. _____

6. _____

7. _____

8. _____

_____

9. _____

_____

10. _____

11. _____

12. _____

_____

13. _____

_____

 12

   **12 – 10 Punkte**  **9 – 7 Punkte**  **6 – 0 Punkte**  **Gesamt-punktzahl**

Vermischte Übungen

1 **Simple past OR past progressive? Translate the following sentences into English. (page 42–45)**

1. Tina arbeitete gerade in ihrem Zimmer, als plötzlich das Licht ausging.

   _____

2. Sie wartete in ihrem Zimmer, als das Telefon klingelte.

   _____

3. Plötzlich ging das Licht wieder an, während sie mit ihrem Freund redete.

   _____

4. Tinas Eltern kamen nach Hause, während Tina ein Computerspiel spielte.

   _____ | 4 |

★ **2** **Rewrite the following sentences: Put the active into the passive and the passive into the active. (page 46–51)**

1. Bob invited the guests last week. _____

2. The invitations were written on the computer by Bob's father. _____

   _____

3. Bob and his mother made all the food. _____

   _____

4. At 10 o'clock Bob's father takes the guests home. _____

   _____ | 4 |

3 **If-clauses: Fill in the correct tense of the verbs. (page 52–57)**

1. If my hobby was golf, I _____ (to get) a lot of fresh air.

2. My mother will buy me new swimsuit if I _____ (to take) part in the school swimming competition.

3. If Deanna played the guitar, she _____ (to join) the school band.

4. I would take more photos if I _____ (to have) a better camera.

5. If I _____ (to feel)) ill, I would drink a glass of hot lemon juice.

6. He _____ (to win) the piano competition if he practised more often.

$\boxed{4}$

4 **Fill in "who" or "which". (page 58–61)**

The disco in our town, _____ is very expensive, is not very good.

The teenagers _____ go there don't like the music because the DJ,

_____ is 34, always plays old songs.

He doesn't play CDs, he plays records _____ are not OK anymore and

sound terrible. The disco's decoration, _____ is older than the

teenagers _____ go there, is very ugly. I would like to find a disco

_____ is nice and inexpensive, but all the others are too far away. And

there is no one _____ can drive me there. Maybe I should stay at

home and read a book.

$\boxed{8}$

5

  20 – 17 Punkte  **16 – 11** Punkte  **10 – 0** Punkte   Gesamt-punktzahl

Autorinnen   Ingrid Preedy und Brigitte Seidl

Bibliografische Information der Deutschen Nationalbibliothek
Die Deutsche Nationalbibliothek verzeichnet diese Publikation in der
Deutschen Nationalbibliografie; detaillierte bibliografische Daten sind
im Internet über http://dnb.dnb.de abrufbar.

1. Auflage

© Duden 2013   J I H
Bibliographisches Institut GmbH
Mecklenburgische Straße 53, 14197 Berlin

Redaktionelle Leitung Anika Donner, Heike Gras
Redaktion Marion Krause
Illustrationen Dorina Tessmann
Herstellung Ursula Fürst
Layout Horst Bachmann
Umschlaggestaltung 2issue, München
Umschlagillustration Dorina Tessmann
Satz Satzpunkt Ursula Ewert GmbH, Bayreuth
Druck und Bindung AZ Druck und Datentechnik GmbH
Heisinger Straße 16, 87437 Kempten
Printed in Germany

ISBN 978-3-411-87140-7